PSALMS FOR LIFE

Chris Palmer

WIPF & STOCK · Eugene, Oregon

Wipf and Stock Publishers
199 W 8th Ave, Suite 3
Eugene, OR 97401

Psalms for Life
By Palmer, Christopher
Copyright©2019 Apostolos
ISBN 13: 978-1-5326-8100-4
Publication date 2/1/2019
Previously published by Apostolos, 2019

Unless otherwise stated, all scripture quotations are from THE HOLY BIBLE, NEW INTERNATIONAL VERSION®, NIV® Copyright © 1973, 1978, 1984, 2011 by Biblica, Inc.® Used by permission. All rights reserved worldwide.

All rights reserved. No part of this book may be reproduced or transmitted in any form or by any means, electronic or mechanical, including photocopying, recording, or by any information storage and retrieval system, without permission in writing from the publisher. The views expressed herein may not necessarily be those of the publisher.

Cover Design by Faithbuilders, London. Cover Images © Jacob Gregory | Dreamstime.com

Psalms for Life: Everyday Living in the Psalms

Who hasn't experienced the highs and lows of everyday life? We have all encountered joy and sadness; good and bad; health and illness; wealth and poverty; friendship and loneliness; security and fear – the normal experiences and emotions of human existence. We often forget that the biblical characters also experienced the full range of human emotions. Their life experiences are recorded in God's word for our help and learning. The Bible is an excellent resource to help us face the joys and trials of life. It assures us of God's ever-present help. Everyday living is best expressed through the writings of the psalmists, a variety of authors who recorded their everyday experiences from which we can learn and be encouraged.

The Book of Psalms ('Psalter,' 'the book of praises,' a word originally used to refer to the variety of stringed instruments used in the Old Testament worship then later applied to the actual songs) contains 150 'songs' of praise and prayer. Each Psalm has its own unique purpose, but they can all be used in private or public worship to express thanksgiving to God and as a manual for nurturing spiritual life. That is, they bring the reader into contact with God in a way that can promote personal reflection and spiritual growth.

Yahweh the God of Israel is the centre of the Psalms because he is the centre of life. Each of the psalmists engages with God in a variety of ways and for a variety of reasons. God is the creator and sustainer of life; the provider of help and support; the source of forgiveness and true happiness; perhaps best summarised in Ps 124:8:

> *Our help is in the name of the LORD, the Maker of heaven and earth.*

As you contemplate life, how much of an influence does God have on your everyday experiences?

"The most valuable thing the Psalms do for me is to express the same delight in God which made David dance."

C. S. Lewis

A Guide to This Book

'Psalms for Life' is a series of 12 studies, one for each month of the year. It provides the reader with the opportunity to share their life experiences with the OT writers and each other.

Each study contains:

- A reading plan for each month.
- A Psalm to read and study during the month.
- A brief outline of the Psalm.
- Questions to aid reflection.
- A prayer.

The purpose of these studies is to allow individuals to engage with the biblical text and think about how the principles contained in God's word can be applied to everyday living.

The reading plan is suggested so that as you read you will be able to relate to many of the everyday emotions which the psalmists encountered. This will encourage you in all the circumstances you face.

Begin your study by reading the Psalm, read it through a few times and make a note of anything that stands out. For example, what does the Psalm say about the character of God, reasons to praise and be thankful, problems faced, relationships, spiritual desire and growth. Your own insights are so helpful to your spiritual growth and enhance group discussion. What is the Psalm saying to you? What can you share with others that has blessed you?

Next read through the outline provided. This is given to highlight the most relevant features of the Psalm and suggest the lessons we can learn from the verses.

The next section is a series of simple questions to help reflection, provoke thought and to direct discussion about the Psalm.

The prayer is a general response to God's dealings with us considering the content of the Psalm and is offered to help direct your prayers.

Happiness in Every Day Life: Psalm 1

January Reading Plan: Psalm 1–12

Read Psalm 1

¹ Blessed is the one who does not walk in step with the wicked or stand in the way that sinners take or sit in the company of mockers, ² but whose delight is in the law of the Lord, and who meditates on his law day and night. ³ That person is like a tree planted by streams of water, which yields its fruit in season and whose leaf does not wither— whatever they do prospers.

⁴ Not so the wicked! They are like chaff that the wind blows away. ⁵ Therefore the wicked will not stand in the judgment, nor sinners in the assembly of the righteous. ⁶ For the Lord watches over the way of the righteous, but the way of the wicked leads to destruction.

Outline

The psalmist states that true happiness or blessing is possible in everyday life. Who doesn't want to be happy? This blessedness is contrasted with the way of life of the 'wicked,' 'sinners,' 'scoffers,' or those who have only ungodly intentions in life (v. 1). However, as the people of God we should desire the help of God and no one else. The psalmist places a great emphasis on the 'law of the Lord' or how the individual should seek direction from God's law (the word of God). This seeking direction for life in the word of God should be a regular habit (v. 2). The person who follows God's ways and abides in him, will experience a life of fulfilment and fruitfulness (v. 3).

This contrasts with the life of the 'wicked' who are like 'chaff' (v. 4) – something worthless that is discarded. The wicked cannot withstand the judgement of God or worship God in truth (v. 5). However, the 'righteous' are known by God and can be assured of his divine help and blessing forever. Those who follow the Lord are assured of their eternal destiny (v. 6). All people face the choice; will they follow the ways of the righteous or the ways of the wicked? Psalm 1 sets out that the righteous (God's people) receive the blessings of God because they are saved and follow his ways. It should be the desire of every disciple of Jesus to seek his blessing and to enjoy the fulness of God in everyday life.

Questions for Reflection

a) Verse 1. Do you desire the blessing of God or are you focussed on other things? (Matt 6:33; 1 Tim 6:6–11)

b) Verse 1. Notice the progression of walking, standing, and sitting. What do you think this means for our lives today? (Prov 4:10–19; 2 Pet 3:17)

c) Verse 3. What do you understand as 'spiritual fruit?' Are you seeing this in your everyday life? (John 15:1–11; Gal 5:22–23)

d) Verse 6. How does this verse bring comfort to the people of God? (John 10:14, 27–29; John 14:1–6)

Notes

Prayer: Thank you, Lord, for your great blessings in my life; help me to experience more of your blessing so I can be a blessing to others. Amen.

Following the Shepherd: Psalm 23

February Reading Plan: Psalm 13–24

Read Psalm 23

[1] The Lord is my shepherd, I lack nothing. [2] He makes me lie down in green pastures, he leads me beside quiet waters, [3] he refreshes my soul. He guides me along the right paths for his name's sake. [4] Even though I walk through the darkest valley, I will fear no evil, for you are with me; your rod and your staff, they comfort me.

[5] You prepare a table before me in the presence of my enemies. You anoint my head with oil; my cup overflows. [6] Surely your goodness and love will follow me all the days of my life, and I will dwell in the house of the Lord forever.

Outline

In this Psalm we are confronted with the identity of the Lord as shepherd of our lives. Shepherds were a common sight in ancient Israel and King David, the writer of this Psalm, had once been a shepherd (Ps 78:70–72); he knew what he was talking about! The picture that David presents of his shepherd 'the Lord' is one we should all treasure.

In verse 1, the shepherd is pictured as providing for the needs of the flock. When we come into a relationship with God, he has our best interests at heart. Verse 2 reminds us that the shepherd supplies good nourishment, refreshment and rest. Verse 3 states that our spiritual restoration is found only through the shepherd's actions for 'he restores my soul.' The one who cares for our souls is also the one who will lead us in the right way, in 'paths of righteousness' (i.e. in those ways which are appropriate to godly living), as ultimately this brings us closer to him. In verse 4 the shepherd who cares and leads also comforts the flock in tough times, just as Jesus has promised to never leave us. However, it is comforting to know the shepherd has a 'rod and staff,' symbols which reassure us of his authority, correction and protection. Verse 5 focusses on the provision of the shepherd for his flock. Sheep have numerous enemies and are easy prey, but the shepherd would provide food and protection from wild animals. And this provision was abundant; our shepherd doesn't deal in half measures but overflowing fullness. The last verse (v. 6) turns our attention to the security which the sheep find in the shepherd. We can have confidence in our shepherd through this life and into eternity. What a deep sense of assurance, comfort and joy is available to all who follow the shepherd.

Questions for Reflection

a) Verse 1. The shepherd is a prominent theme in the biblical narrative. What image does it produce in your mind? (2 Sam 5:2; Ezek 34:1–10)

b) Verse 1. Is the Lord your shepherd and are you following him faithfully? (Mark 1:17; Matt 16:24)

c) Verse 1–3. What benefits are there from following the Shepherd? (John 10:10; 1 Pet 5:4)

d) Verses 4–5. Where do you turn in the difficult days; how has the Lord proven to be your Shepherd at these times? (John 16:33; John 14:16–27)

Notes

Prayer: Lord I thank you that you are my shepherd and all I need is found by simply trusting in you as my saviour, guide, and reward. Amen.

My Times are in God's Hands: Psalm 31

March Reading Plan: Psalm 25–37

Read Psalm 31 (extract below)

¹ In you, Lord, I have taken refuge; let me never be put to shame; deliver me in your righteousness. ² Turn your ear to me, come quickly to my rescue; be my rock of refuge, a strong fortress to save me. ³ Since you are my rock and my fortress, for the sake of your name lead and guide me. ⁴ Keep me free from the trap that is set for me, for you are my refuge. ⁵ Into your hands I commit my spirit; deliver me, Lord, my faithful God. ¹⁴ But I trust in you, Lord; I say, "You are my God." ¹⁵ My times are in your hands; deliver me from the hands of my enemies, from those who pursue me. ¹⁶ Let your face shine on your servant; save me in your unfailing love. ¹⁷ Let me not be put to shame, Lord, for I have cried out to you; but let the wicked be put to shame and be silent in the realm of the dead. ¹⁸ Let their lying lips be silenced, for with pride and contempt they speak arrogantly against the righteous. ¹⁹ How abundant are the good things that you have stored up for those who fear you, that you bestow in the sight of all, on those who take refuge in you. ²⁰ In the shelter of your presence you hide them from all human intrigues; you keep them safe in your dwelling from accusing tongues. ²¹ Praise be to the Lord, for he showed me the wonders of his love when I was in a city under siege. ²² In my alarm I said, "I am cut off from your sight!" Yet you heard my cry for mercy when I called to you for help. ²³ Love the Lord, all his faithful people! The Lord preserves those who are true to him, but the proud he pays back in full. ²⁴ Be strong and take heart, all you who hope in the Lord.

Outline

Trust is an important part of our lives. Who do we trust? Who has our best interests at heart? Where can we turn when we need help? This Psalm encourages us as we reflect on the fact that we can trust God in all our situations. Our lives are in God's hands (v. 15). This should cause us to have confidence in God as he leads and directs us through life. The psalmist was going through a very difficult period as his enemies were plotting against him even to the point threatening his life (v. 13). However, whatever was going on around him, and whoever was against him, the Lord was his refuge, strength and protection. Verses 1–5 remind us how we must face every situation by recognising the ability of God to offer refuge, strength and protection in life. Verse 5 reminds us of the conscious decision we must make to place our 'spirit' (life) into God's hands. Verses 6–13 present a picture of those who are out to destroy the psalmist and end his rule as king of Israel.

Opposition is often an aspect of our Christian lives which can lead to physical, emotional and spiritual weariness. Yet, despite the outer threats, verses 14–18 reassure us that if we trust God he will see us through the most difficult of situations. As followers of God we must call out to him for his help in our lives. Verses 19–24 conclude the Psalm with a recognition of the greatness, goodness, and love of God which should cause us to praise him and rely on his strength and his ability to keep us strong in the most difficult of times. What a great privilege it is to know that; 'my times are in Your hands.'

Questions for Reflection

a) Verses 1–4. Why do we need to trust God? (Isa 32:1–2; Isa 41:8–14)

b) Verse 5. Have you placed your life completely (100%) in God's hands? (Isa 64:8; Matt 11:28–29)

c) Verses 14–18. How do you cope with the stresses and strains of life? (Ps 33:18; 2 Cor 12:8–10)

d) Verses 19–24. How do you react to knowing such a good God? (1 Tim 1:12–17; Rev 5:8–14)

Notes

_____

_____

_____

_____

_____

_____

_____

_____

_____

Prayer: Thank you, Lord, for your great blessings in my life. Help me to experience more of your blessing so I can be a blessing to others. Amen.

Taste and See That the Lord is Good: Psalm 34

April Reading Plan: Psalm 38–50

Read Psalm 34

[1] I will extol the Lord at all times; his praise will always be on my lips. [2] I will glory in the Lord; let the afflicted hear and rejoice. [3] Glorify the Lord with me; let us exalt his name together. [4] I sought the Lord, and he answered me; he delivered me from all my fears. [5] Those who look to him are radiant; their faces are never covered with shame. [6] This poor man called, and the Lord heard him; he saved him out of all his troubles. [7] The angel of the Lord encamps around those who fear him, and he delivers them. [8] Taste and see that the Lord is good; blessed is the one who takes refuge in him. ... [15] The eyes of the Lord are on the righteous, and his ears are attentive to their cry; [16] but the face of the Lord is against those who do evil, to blot out their name from the earth. [17] The righteous cry out, and the Lord hears them; he delivers them from all their troubles. [18] The Lord is close to the brokenhearted and saves those who are crushed in spirit. [19] The righteous person may have many troubles, but the Lord delivers him from them all; [20] he protects all his bones, not one of them will be broken. [21] Evil will slay the wicked; the foes of the righteous will be condemned. [22] The Lord will rescue his servants; no one who takes refuge in him will be condemned.

Outline

Tasty food makes us feel happy! The beautiful taste causes us to want more and to tell others the recipe or restaurant where we ate. The psalmist encourages others to 'taste and see that the Lord is good' (v. 8). His first-hand experience of trusting the Lord had caused him to know that the Lord is good. Verses 1–3 he simply wants to praise the Lord because as v 4 tells us the Lord had answered his prayers. Believers have a privileged position because when we pray, God listens. The deliverance God gave the psalmist brought praise flowing from his lips. How easy do we find it to praise the Lord? Verses 6–7 emphasise that the Lord saves those who cry out to him in trouble. The psalmist's confidence in the Lord continues throughout the Psalm; in verse 10 the Lord's provision is mentioned; in verses 15–17 the Lord is always listening to our cries for help; in verse 18 there is a genuine concern for those in a state of grief. Verses 19–21 tell us that however tough things may be the Lord is always present to keep the righteous (his people), in security. The culmination comes in v 21, where we see the true purposes of the Lord's dealings with humanity. The Lord wants to redeem our souls;

that is, deliver them eternally if we will simply come to him in trust and submission. As verse 8 puts it, the one who takes refuge in the Lord will be truly blessed. There is no condemnation for those who are in Christ (Rom 8:1). The psalmist had a great confidence in the eternal nature and care of God for his people; this all stemmed from his experiences of God and that he had 'tasted' the goodness of God and knew divine blessing.

Questions for Reflection

a) Verse 8. Have you tasted the goodness of God? (Ps 107:8; John 6:35–40)

b) Verse 8. Has what you have tasted caused you to want others to experience the same goodness? (Mark 4:18–20; John 4:25–42)

c) Verse 8. Are you pursuing happiness (blessed) in life what means are you employing to find that happiness? (Matt 6:33; John 10:10)

d) Verses 15–21. Whatever situation you are dealing with at present remember the Lord is there to hear and save. (Ps 50:15; Heb 7:25)

Notes

Prayer: Lord I thank you that I have tasted of your goodness. Please help me to encourage others to experience your goodness. Amen.

Enjoying God's Provision: Psalm 37

May Reading Plan: Psalm 51–63

Read Psalm 37 (extract below)

¹ Do not fret because of those who are evil or be envious of those who do wrong; ² for like the grass they will soon wither, like green plants they will soon die away. ³ Trust in the Lord and do good; dwell in the land and enjoy safe pasture. ⁴ Take delight in the Lord, and he will give you the desires of your heart. ⁵ Commit your way to the Lord; trust in him and he will do this: ⁶ He will make your righteous reward shine like the dawn, your vindication like the noonday sun. ⁷ Be still before the Lord and wait patiently for him; do not fret when people succeed in their ways, when they carry out their wicked schemes. ⁸ Refrain from anger and turn from wrath; do not fret—it leads only to evil. ⁹ For those who are evil will be destroyed, but those who hope in the Lord will inherit the land. ¹⁰ A little while, and the wicked will be no more; though you look for them, they will not be found. ¹¹ But the meek will inherit the land and enjoy peace and prosperity. ¹² The wicked plot against the righteous and gnash their teeth at them; ¹³ but the Lord laughs at the wicked, for he knows their day is coming.

Outline

This Psalm sets out who will enjoy the blessings of God. In the OT context this means Israel (vv. 9,11,22,29), who will inherit the promised land, live in it and experience all God's blessings. The security of knowing and enjoying God's provision was paramount in the experience of the psalmist. There are five simple aspects that will help as we endeavour to enjoy God's provision:

1. Verse 3. We must trust in the Lord, with hearts and minds fixed on God. Trust means to have confidence and hope in God alone.

2. Verse 4. We must delight in the Lord and seek our happiness in God alone. Nothing else should crowd the Lord out of our lives.

3. Verse 5. We must commit our ways to the Lord. Commit here means 'to roll our burdens on God;' life need not be a burden as we can take everything to God in prayer and confidence.

4. Verse 7. We must rest in the Lord. This means to 'be still' or wait. There are situations in life that we sometimes think need a faster response and immediate action. However, God says simply 'wait my time, don't get anxious I'm in control.'

5. Verse 11. We must humble ourselves before God. This is a summary of all the preceding elements as it means placing ourselves completely in God's hands.

Questions for Reflection

a) Verse 3. Are you trusting the Lord convinced he is able to help you? (Rom 8:38; Phil 1:6)

b) Verse 4. Is the Lord your delight or do other things hold your attention? (Ps 73:25; Luke 12:13–21)

c) Verse 5. Have you committed your whole life to God? (Matt 7:13–14, 24–27; 1 Pet 5:7)

d) Verse 7. Waiting on God is essential. What do you see as the art of waiting on God? (Isa 40:31; Matt 6:5–8)

Notes

_____
_____
_____
_____
_____
_____
_____
_____
_____
_____

Prayer: Lord I want to enjoy your provision. Please help me to trust in you totally and seek all my fulfilment in you alone. Amen.

Desiring God: Psalm 42

June Reading Plan: Psalm 64–76

Read Psalm 42

¹ As the deer pants for streams of water, so my soul pants for you, my God. ² My soul thirsts for God, for the living God. When can I go and meet with God? ³ My tears have been my food day and night, while people say to me all day long, "Where is your God?" ⁴ These things I remember as I pour out my soul: how I used to go to the house of God under the protection of the Mighty One with shouts of joy and praise among the festive throng. ⁵ Why, my soul, are you downcast? Why so disturbed within me? Put your hope in God, for I will yet praise him, my Savior and my God. ⁶ My soul is downcast within me; therefore I will remember you from the land of the Jordan, the heights of Hermon—from Mount Mizar. ⁷ Deep calls to deep in the roar of your waterfalls; all your waves and breakers have swept over me. ⁸ By day the Lord directs his love, at night his song is with me—a prayer to the God of my life. ⁹ I say to God my Rock, "Why have you forgotten me? Why must I go about mourning, oppressed by the enemy?" ¹⁰ My bones suffer mortal agony as my foes taunt me, saying to me all day long, "Where is your God?" ¹¹ Why, my soul, are you downcast? Why so disturbed within me? Put your hope in God, for I will yet praise him, my Savior and my God.

Outline

'Down but not out!' This is how the psalmist must have felt as he penned the words of Psalm 42. Today we might label his experience 'spiritual depression.' The psalmist was away from Jerusalem (v. 3) and away from the house of God (v. 4). This had caused him grief and tears (v. 3); his soul was in anguish (vv. 5–6, 9–11) his situation had driven him to the point of despair. However, he had one source of hope God himself v 1, his situation was so desperate, yet he simply desired God as he knew his God can make the difference to his dire situation. To him God was the source of spiritual refreshing, his spiritual drought can be quenched by an encounter with the living God (v. 1). The picture is portrayed of a wild animal fleeing the hunter and knowing if it can just get a cooling refreshing drink it'll make its escape to freedom. The psalmist knows God will quench his inner longings and desires. Not only does he desire refreshing he also desires stability, and in verse 9 we find that God is a rock upon which he can know security and safety. God as 'rock' is the source of unfailing strength, dependability, power, safety, protection and security. Jesus Christ is the great foundation stone on which we can build our lives and know that protection from the storms of life. The psalmist reminds us in verse 2 that we must have a genuine desire for God; and in verses 5 and 11, we find that the secret to all of life's difficulties is to hope in God. Our Christian experience can suffer due to a loss of desire; however, revival is possible if we begin to seek God and experience his spiritual refreshing.

Questions for Reflection

a) Verse 1. Why should we thirst after God? (Isa 55:1; John 7:37–39)

b) Verses 3–6. What is your reaction to times of 'spiritual depression' or anxiety? (Ps 10:11–12; Phil 4:6–7)

c) Verse 9. How are your spiritual foundations? Do they require attention? (Ps 18:1–3; Matt 7:24–27)

d) Is there a need for a time of refreshing or revival in your heart today? How may this be achieved? (Ps 85:6; Acts 3:19)

Notes

_____
_____
_____
_____
_____
_____
_____
_____
_____
_____
_____

Prayer: Lord here I am, revive me, refresh me, renew me so that I may have a greater desire for you and focus all my hope in you alone. Amen.

The God of Jacob: Psalm 46

July Reading Plan: Psalm 77–90

Read Psalm 46

¹ God is our refuge and strength, an ever-present help in trouble. ² Therefore we will not fear, though the earth give way and the mountains fall into the heart of the sea, ³ though its waters roar and foam and the mountains quake with their surging. ⁴ There is a river whose streams make glad the city of God, the holy place where the Most High dwells. ⁵ God is within her, she will not fall; God will help her at break of day. ⁶ Nations are in uproar, kingdoms fall; he lifts his voice, the earth melts. ⁷ The Lord Almighty is with us; the God of Jacob is our fortress. ⁸ Come and see what the Lord has done, the desolations he has brought on the earth. ⁹ He makes wars cease to the ends of the earth. He breaks the bow and shatters the spear; he burns the shields with fire. ¹⁰ He says, "Be still, and know that I am God; I will be exalted among the nations, I will be exalted in the earth." ¹¹ The Lord Almighty is with us; the God of Jacob is our fortress.

Outline

This is possibly one of the best loved Psalms, as it introduces the reader to the certainty of the help of God in all situations. What a great confidence to us to know God is with us. Verses 1–3 remind us that God is a refuge for all his people; someone who is there to help in the problems of life. The description is graphic as it may appear that the whole of the created order is disappearing, which is probably an image of the difficulties facing Israel at that time. However, the Lord God is still in control. This tumultuous picture is contrasted to the peaceful running of a river (vv. 4–5) which brings refreshment, life, and happiness to the citizens. Interestingly, Jerusalem does not have a river running through it, however, God is the one who brings refreshing and blessing to his people. In order for the blessings of God to be on his people, he must be the centre of their lives. As disciples of Jesus we must know that God is in the centre of our lives. He is the only source of true blessing especially amidst the turmoil of life. Verses 6–9 reiterate the power of God who stands firm against the opposition of the world and how God will have the ultimate victory. Verses 10–11 tell how God will break in to history he will simply say 'enough!' or 'be still, stop striving because all people must know that I am God and there is no other.' Jacob's/Israel's God is the one revealed as Immanuel, 'God with us.' He commands the hosts of heaven and is on the side of his people. Therefore, all God's people can rest in his divine protection and provision.

Questions for Reflection

a) Verses 1–3. When have you needed to know God as your place of refuge and strength? (Ps 28:6–9; Rom 8:28)

b) Verses 4–5. Is God at the centre of your life? Why do you believe that this is necessary? (Jas 4:13–15; 2 Pet 1:2–4)

c) Verses 10–11. Are you too busy to hear from God; is it time to stop and focus on God? (Ps 25:4–5; Luke 10:40–42)

d) It's in the stillness that we can know the blessings of God; take some time to focus on God and be refreshed. (1 Kgs 19:4–12; Mark 6:31–32)

Notes

_____
_____
_____
_____
_____
_____
_____
_____
_____
_____
_____
_____

Prayer: Lord I thank you that you are there for me as a shelter in the storm. Your refreshing of my life gives me confidence in your sovereign control of all things. Amen.

Joy – Lost and Found: Psalm 51

August Reading Plan: Psalm 91–102

Read Psalm 51 (extract below)

[1] Have mercy on me, O God, according to your unfailing love; according to your great compassion blot out my transgressions. [2] Wash away all my iniquity and cleanse me from my sin. [3] For I know my transgressions, and my sin is always before me. [4] Against you, you only, have I sinned and done what is evil in your sight; so you are right in your verdict and justified when you judge. [5] Surely I was sinful at birth, sinful from the time my mother conceived me. ... [7] Cleanse me with hyssop, and I will be clean; wash me, and I will be whiter than snow. [8] Let me hear joy and gladness; let the bones you have crushed rejoice. [9] Hide your face from my sins and blot out all my iniquity. [10] Create in me a pure heart, O God, and renew a steadfast spirit within me. [11] Do not cast me from your presence or take your Holy Spirit from me. [12] Restore to me the joy of your salvation and grant me a willing spirit, to sustain me. [13] Then I will teach transgressors your ways, so that sinners will turn back to you. ... [17] My sacrifice, O God, is a broken spirit; a broken and contrite heart you, God, will not despise.

Outline

David wrote Psalm 51 during a dark episode in his life – the adulterous affair with Bathsheba and the murder of her innocent husband Uriah (2 Sam 11). The king had lost his joy in God for he had slipped from the narrow path and committed two severe sins: adultery and murder. This Psalm is a prayer for restoration. David is seeking God's forgiveness as he recognised his own failings. He depends on the Lord for salvation. Verses 1–4 remind us that when we sin, God is the one who is offended, and we can only seek forgiveness from him. God is the only one who can wash, cleanse, purge, blot out and forget our sins. Verses 5–9 our human condition is naturally contrary to what God desires. God desires truth and purity, we live under the influence of a fallen nature whereby sin is our natural choice. However, God can take the sinful nature we possess and change it by cleansing us and forgiving us of our sins. Verses 10–17 recognise that since only God can forgive, cleanse, and restore, we must come honestly before him recognising our own unworthiness and inability to save ourselves. God is faithful and will forgive and forget our sin and lead us on to greater things in his service and for his glory. Verses 18–19 offer a prayer for Jerusalem. David wanted his home city to pulsate with the true worship of God. How desperate are we for our home towns to know the truth of forgiveness and the joy of salvation?

Questions for Reflection

a) Verse 4. Have you recognised that sin mars you and causes you to lose your joy in God? (Rom 6:23; 1 John 1:8)

b) Verse 10. God has promised to forgive all your sins. Are you willing to admit your sin and ask for forgiveness? (1 John 1:9; 1 John 2:1–2)

c) Verse 12. What things bring you joy? Does knowing the Lord's salvation cause ultimate joy in your life? (Phil 4:3–4; Jas 1:2–4)

d) Verses 16–17. Humility is a hallmark of the genuine disciple. Are you willing to give your whole self to God thereby allowing him to bring you the true joy of salvation? (2 Chron 7:14; 1 Pet 5:4–7)

Notes

_____
_____
_____
_____
_____
_____
_____
_____
_____
_____
_____
_____

Prayer: Lord I realise I am nothing but a sinful soul in need of your constant forgiveness. Forgive my sin and let me know your joy. Amen.

Learning from the Past: Psalm 77

September Reading Plan: Psalm 103–115

Read Psalm 77 (extract below)

[1] I cried out to God for help; I cried out to God to hear me. [2] When I was in distress, I sought the Lord; at night I stretched out untiring hands, and I would not be comforted. ... [4] You kept my eyes from closing; I was too troubled to speak. [5] I thought about the former days, the years of long ago; [6] I remembered my songs in the night. My heart meditated and my spirit asked: [7] "Will the Lord reject forever? Will he never show his favor again? [8] Has his unfailing love vanished forever? Has his promise failed for all time? [9] Has God forgotten to be merciful? Has he in anger withheld his compassion?" [10] Then I thought, "To this I will appeal: the years when the Most High stretched out his right hand. [11] I will remember the deeds of the Lord; yes, I will remember your miracles of long ago. [12] I will consider all your works and meditate on all your mighty deeds."

Outline

Have you ever felt that God is not there for you and is not hearing let alone answering your prayer? You are not alone! The writer of Psalm 77 experienced the same feelings. Yet even though he faced a challenging situation and spiritual opposition he reflected on the past, and this gave him strength for the present. It is good at times to consider God's past dealings with us for they made us what we are today. Experiences, good or bad, mould and shape us into the people we are in God. Sometimes we need to stop when in doubt, anxiety or fear, and look back at God's dealings with us, taking heart for he has never left us. It's good to reflect on how God dealt with us to bring about his plans and purposes. Verses 1–9 offer a summary of how the psalmist felt. He was anxious, as God appeared silent, inactive, and unresponsive to his frequent desperate prayers. However, verses 10–20 show a change of heart, as the thought of God's mighty acts on behalf of Israel in the past gave him courage. God will not forsake his people. Verse 15 reveals the psalmist's hope; God redeemed his people from Egypt and led them through the wilderness to the promised land. It is only God who can redeem us, keep, provide and fulfil his plans and purposes for us; all his people must do is keep calling on him and wait patiently for his deliverance.

Questions for Reflection

a) Verses 1–4. Are you calling on God for a specific unresolved situation? Keep calling. Be persistent and hope in God. (Ps 50:15; Dan 10:12–13)

b) Verses 11–20. What lessons have you learned about God through his past dealings with you? Has this changed your understanding of God and self? (Rom 15:4; 1 Cor 10:6,11)

c) Verse 12. Do you meditate on God and his works in your life? What effect does this have on your discipleship? (1 Tim 4:15–16; Phil 4:8)

d) Verses 15–20. You trusted God for salvation – why not share something of your spiritual journey with others in your group, remembering that it is God who has led you all the way. (Acts 22:3–21)

Notes

Prayer: Lord I thank you for the work you have done in my life. It is good to know that I can continually trust in you. Amen.

Help from the Lord: Psalm 86

October Reading Plan: Psalm 116–123

Read Psalm 86 (extract below)

[1] Hear me, Lord, and answer me, for I am poor and needy. [2] Guard my life, for I am faithful to you; save your servant who trusts in you. You are my God; [3] have mercy on me, Lord, for I call to you all day long. [4] Bring joy to your servant, Lord, for I put my trust in you. [5] You, Lord, are forgiving and good, abounding in love to all who call to you. [6] Hear my prayer, Lord; listen to my cry for mercy. [7] When I am in distress, I call to you, because you answer me. [8] Among the gods there is none like you, Lord; no deeds can compare with yours. [9] All the nations you have made will come and worship before you, Lord; they will bring glory to your name. [10] For you are great and do marvelous deeds; you alone are God. [11] Teach me your way, Lord, that I may rely on your faithfulness; give me an undivided heart, that I may fear your name. [12] I will praise you, Lord my God, with all my heart; I will glorify your name forever. [13] For great is your love toward me; you have delivered me from the depths, from the realm of the dead.

Outline

This beautiful Psalm is a prayer for the Lord's help in times of trouble. The psalmists, perhaps more than any other biblical writers, were happy to express their inadequacies and their need of God's help. We should never be afraid to seek God's help in any situation. If it's important to us, it's important to God! God is there and desires to hear our calls, so we can know the intervention we need. This Psalm teaches us how to pray. Firstly, we are encouraged to make the correct approach to God (v. 1). 'Lord' is the true designation of the one we seek; Jehovah the self-existent, eternal one. What a privilege to be able to approach the creator God and bring our petitions to him. Throughout the Psalm we see several references to the Lord. We can approach the Lord because of his nature and character (v. 3) 'the Lord is gracious.' It is also good to know that the Lord is good, ready to forgive and loving (v. 5); the Lord is listening (v. 6); the Lord is unique (v. 8); the Lord is to be worshipped (v. 9); the Lord is the source of truth (v. 11); the Lord is merciful, patient and loving (v. 15); the Lord is a constant source of support and help in life (v. 17). When we consider the Lord as the psalmist does here it should cause us to have great confidence in God and be intent on going to the Lord for his help in the times of trouble. But also, never forget to thank the Lord for his help and for his great salvation (vv. 12–13).

Questions for Reflection

a) Verse 1. When you pray how do you approach the Lord? Why do you approach him in such a manner? (Matt 6:9; Eph 3:14–15)

b) Verse 2. When you pray how do you see yourself? (Luke 18:10–14)

c) Verse 7. Days of trouble do come what is your first reaction to those challenging times? (Ps 50:15; Jonah 2:1–9)

d) Verses 8–10. Why do you have confidence in the Lord? (Acts 27:22–25; Heb 1:1–4)

Notes

_____
_____
_____
_____
_____
_____
_____
_____
_____
_____
_____
_____
_____

Prayer: Lord I thank you that you have guaranteed that you will be there for me in the day of trouble. I praise you for how you have helped me in the past and I trust you for all that is ahead. Amen.

Praise Every Day: Psalm 103

November Reading Plan: Psalm 124–136

Read Psalm 103 (extract below)

¹ Praise the Lord, my soul; all my inmost being, praise his holy name. ² Praise the Lord, my soul, and forget not all his benefits—³ who forgives all your sins and heals all your diseases, ⁴ who redeems your life from the pit and crowns you with love and compassion, ⁵ who satisfies your desires with good things so that your youth is renewed like the eagle's. ⁶ The Lord works righteousness and justice for all the oppressed. ⁷ He made known his ways to Moses, his deeds to the people of Israel: ⁸ The Lord is compassionate and gracious, slow to anger, abounding in love. ⁹ He will not always accuse, nor will he harbor his anger forever; ¹⁰ he does not treat us as our sins deserve or repay us according to our iniquities. ¹¹ For as high as the heavens are above the earth, so great is his love for those who fear him; ¹² as far as the east is from the west, so far has he removed our transgressions from us. ¹³ As a father has compassion on his children, so the Lord has compassion on those who fear him; ¹⁴ for he knows how we are formed, he remembers that we are dust.

Outline

We are often lax in praising the Lord. The psalmists were people who loved to praise (Psalms is a 'book of praises.') It's good to praise the Lord and be thankful for all he has achieved in our lives. Praise should be a daily occurrence in the life of a true disciple. Psalm 103 sets out some reasons why we should praise the Lord. Verses 1 and 22 envelope the Psalm in praise as the psalmist encourages himself to praise the Lord. True praise is not induced by nice songs but by a deep inner realisation of the work of God in one's soul. This is seen in verses 3–14 where the results of salvation are recognised. Praise begins in the soul of the individual whose sin has been dealt with by God. The realisation of this should bring joy to the heart and praise to the lips. Verse 3 presents God as a compassionate forgiving Lord who has redeemed us (v. 4), who satisfies and renews us (v. 5), and who is compassionate (v. 8). He has not dealt with us as we deserve (v. 10) but has removed our sins (v. 12) for he loves us as a true father (v. 13). It is important that we recognise our mortality (vv. 15–16) as this reinforces our need of the immortal God, the only source of eternal life. As verse 17 reminds us, God's love has eternal consequences – there is no other means of knowing eternal life. Let's praise the Lord because he is sovereign, ruling from heaven and in complete control of our lives (v. 19). As we consider the Lord's attributes and works it is impossible not to praise him for his goodness to us.

Questions for Reflection

a) Verse 1. What do you define as 'praise?' Do you require external stimuli to produce praise or can you praise the Lord in any situation? (Acts 3:8; Acts 16:25)

b) Verses 2–5. Why should we praise the Lord? (Eph 2:4–9; Col 2:13–14)

c) Verses 10–12. How deeply does the realisation of forgiveness affect your life and praise? (Luke 15:7; 19:8–10)

d) Being forgiven, we should forgive. Is there someone you need to forgive to release God's blessing in your life? (Matt 18:21–35; Eph 4:32)

Notes

Prayer: Thank you Lord for all your blessings in my life. Help me to praise you for all the things you have done for me. Amen.

Unity Brings Blessing: Psalm 133

December Reading Plan: Psalm 137–150

Read Psalm 133

¹ How good and pleasant it is when God's people live together in unity! ² It is like precious oil poured on the head, running down on the beard, running down on Aaron's beard, down on the collar of his robe. ³ It is as if the dew of Hermon were falling on Mount Zion. For there the Lord bestows his blessing, even life forevermore.

Outline

The biblical principle of unity is often neglected. It is possible for Christians to pay lip service to the importance of unity without seeking to maintain it in church life. The biblical narrative promotes unity throughout and focusses the attention on the standard expected by God. Psalm 133 is a great 'spiritual barometer' in respect to unity in the Christian community and provides a framework around which a strong united people can be built. The psalmist reminds the reader that the pursuit of unity is 'good and pleasant' or attractive or beautiful (v. 1). As a result, it should be emphasised and sought out. It can attract others to the church. The writer then gives two illustrations of the impact of unity. In verse 2 it is compared to the oil used to anoint the High Priest; this speaks of the consecrated nature of the service of the priests. They had to be totally consecrated to God or cleansed and set apart for spiritual ministry. Those who are called to follow the Lord are set apart for spiritual service and unity is an important aspect of this consecration. Verse 3 relates unity to morning dew which stimulates growth on the mountains of Northern Israel. Mount Hermon is renowned for experiencing a heavy dew that waters the surrounding farm lands and produces luxuriant growth. The united church will be a fruitful church, for as the church is united so it will grow both spiritually and numerically. The final proof of unity is the blessing of God upon his people, here seen in the great promise of 'life' that is divine life within the church, which will affect the wider community and be fulfilled in eternity.

Questions for Reflection

a) Verse 1. Do you recognise the necessity of unity in the church? Why do you believe it is important? (Matt 12:25; Phil 2:1–4)

b) Verse 1. It is not good to simply pay 'lip service' to unity. Are you truly united with the others in your fellowship what can you do to enhance the unity of the fellowship? (Phil 4:2; Heb 13:1)

c) Verse 2. Unity is a spiritual issue. We should seek the Holy Spirit to help bring us closer together and be more effective. (John 14:16–21; 17:11)

d) Verse 3. Is the church fruitful? If not, then perhaps there are issues of disunity which need to be dealt with quickly. (Matt 5:21–24; 18:15–20)

Notes

Prayer: Lord unite your church to make us more effective. If I am causing any disunity, please help me to deal with my wrong attitudes and seek forgiveness from my brothers or sisters. Amen

Further Notes

www.ingramcontent.com/pod-product-compliance
Lightning Source LLC
Chambersburg PA
CBHW061316040426
42444CB00010B/2672